LifeCoach™
Your Teens

FIVE PRINCIPLES TO HELP YOUR KIDS THRIVE

ROGER CROSS

InterVarsity Press
Downers Grove, Illinois

IInterVarsity Press
P.O. Box 1400, Downers Grove, IL 60515-1426
World Wide Web: www.ivpress.com
E-mail: mail@ivpress.com

LifeCoach™ is a trademark owned by Youth for Christ/USA for which an application for
registration has been filed with the United States Patent and Trademark Office, Washington D.C.

InterVarsity Press® is the book-publishing division of InterVarsity Christian Fellowship/USA®, a
student movement active on campus at hundreds of universities, colleges and schools of nursing in
the United States of America, and a member movement of the International Fellowship of
Evangelical Students. For information about local and regional activities, write Public Relations
Dept., InterVarsity Christian Fellowship/USA, 6400 Schroeder Rd., P.O. Box 7895, Madison, WI
53707-7895, or visit the IVCF website at <www.intervarsity.org>.

All Scripture quotations, unless otherwise indicated, are taken from the Holy Bible, New
International Version®. NIV®. Copyright ©1973, 1978, 1984 by International Bible Society.
Used by permission of Zondervan Publishing House. All rights reserved.

Design: Cindy Kiple

Images: Rich Frishman/Getty Images

ISBN 0-8308-3252-1

Printed in the United States of America ∞

Library of Congress Cataloging-in-Publication Data

Cross, Roger, 1943-
    LifeCoach your teens: five principles to help your kids thrive /
Roger Cross.
      p. cm.
    ISBN 0-8308-3252-1 (cloth: alk. paper)
    1. Parenting—Religious aspects—Christianity. 2.
Teenagers—Religious life. I. Title: Life Coach your teens. II.
Title.
BV4529.C76 2004
248.8'45—dc22
                                                                2004004356

| P | 16 | 15 | 14 | 13 | 12 | 11 | 10 | 9 | 8 | 7 | 6 | 5 | 4 | 3 | 2 | 1 |
| Y | 17 | 16 | 15 | 14 | 13 | 12 | 11 | 10 | 09 | 08 | 07 | 06 | 05 | 04 |

*This book is dedicated to the faithful
and deeply committed women and men
of Youth for Christ around the world.
Every day they live out
the principles presented here.*

*I also want to gratefully acknowledge
Lynn Wilford Scarborough,
who was instrumental in helping develop the
early stages of the manuscript.*

Contents

1 **Your Toughest Job**

There are some tough jobs in our world:

stunt double for a pro wrestler, travel agent for Titanic Cruise Lines, air conditioner salesperson in Greenland.

But if you're a parent of a teenager or an out-of-control three-year-old you probably already agree with the title to this chapter. Being a parent has wonderful rewards, but often it is just plain hard work.

I have a friend who laughs when he says, "Grandchildren are your reward for not killing your own kids." I can laugh with him because I've certainly felt the frustration and anger in parenting that would elicit that kind of statement. Come on now, hasn't some form of that declaration crossed your mind as well? It's normal because sometimes as a parent you just don't know what to do. Extreme action seems like the only choice left.

Besides that, what training did we have before we got into this? We all had a parent or parents but we weren't watching very closely when we were growing up. And the truth is that our parents weren't trained well either.

If you're a parent, facing the tough situations just comes with the territory. After all, it's not like you can walk away or just give your kids to someone else to raise. What you need are some practical suggestions on how to make it through the tough times. That's where I'd like to help.

A LITTLE EXPERIENCE— A LOT OF HARD KNOCKS

I think it may be helpful for you to know some of my background. I certainly don't come as an "expert," but I've seen parenting from a number of different angles. And I've learned a ton from my own mistakes.

I had served in ministry as executive director of Ventura County Youth for Christ nearly five years before my wife, Jan, and I had our first child. During those early years I had many conversations with parents who thought I knew something about parenting because I was in youth work. Little did they know that any advice I gave them probably came from some book somewhere.

Six years and one miscarriage later we had our second

child. Like most young parents we were scrambling to make ends meet, balance busy schedules and learn about parenting on the fly. In the meantime, my ministry experience was raising some new questions about how parents relate to their kids. Because our work is primarily with teenagers, I was facing more and more parents who were facing the struggles of the teenage years. Their teenagers were beginning to "spread their wings," and that brought fear. Often the parents would respond by "tightening down the screws," and that seemed to produce the opposite effect of what they desired.

As our first daughter reached the teenage cycle, Jan and I began to experience what other parents were facing. "How late does our daughter stay out? What about dating? Designer clothes?" My experience in working with kids provided some helpful insights, but I quickly lost any resemblance to an "expert" on teenagers. Numerous situations arose that hadn't been addressed in any books I'd read, and I just didn't have any answers.

When our oldest daughter was sixteen and our youngest was ten, we took a seventeen-year-old boy in to live with us. He has become a wonderful part of our family. And while most families don't take in a foster son, the kind of issues we had to face with him are common to parenting.

The reason for this brief look into the Cross history is to help you realize that we're just like millions of other families. I realize my experience in youth work is helpful, but even that just made me more aware of how much I didn't know.

Parenting is often an inch-by-inch experience—two steps forward and one step back, or the reverse. It's failing and learning. Over and over again. Doing some things right, some things wrong. Even in this day of super technology there is no icon I can click on my computer that will give me all the answers.

Out of this experience I offer some practical principles to help you succeed in one of the world's toughest jobs.

TOUGH JOB—TOUGH ENVIRONMENT

If parenting is a tough job, then helping your teenager thrive in school is taking on their toughest environment.

Schools can be brutal. It's undoubtedly one of the reasons the homeschool movement has flourished. Please understand, my purpose is not to attack the educational system. I have many wonderful friends who are doing a great job there. But even they would admit that often the school system does not represent the kind of values that many of us share. My purpose is to give you some practical principles on how to help your teenager navigate this environment.

Your teenager probably spends seven to nine hours a day in school or school-related activities. That's a lot more time than they spend with you. According to a 1999 study by the Phillips Consumer Group, American teens spend 40 percent less time with their parents today than they did in the 1960s. The majority of them claim they spend less than thirty minutes a day talking with their parents. This means that the school environment is probably one of the biggest influences—if not *the* biggest—in your teenager's life.

In this school battlefield one of the landmines is fashion. Even though school is much more about the future than fashion, there's no doubt that the campus is a place to strut your stuff. The halls have turned into a "battle of the brands" and shopping malls have become the town halls of the millennial generation (those born after 1982). Driven by "must haves" and fifty ways to show your midriff, teenagers and their parents spend countless hours and dollars trying to get the "right stuff." Fashion nowadays is more than clothes. It's also about having the right techno toys and transportation devices.

Another landmine is academic pressure. Our current generation of young people faces something different than previous generations. The job market is different and tougher. The pressure to be toward the top of the class is more pronounced. Getting into colleges and universities is more competitive. This pressure is often connected to a teen's desire to have the kind of money that they see as critical to maintain their lifestyle, the most materialistic in our nation's history. Academic pressure, coupled with parental pressure, may explain why two out of three teenagers say it's okay to cheat on exams.

Unfortunately, school is also a place where your teenager can be exposed to illicit drugs, alcohol, pornography and violence—all potential deadly landmines. It may not happen in the classroom, but many young people are first exposed to these kind of activities through school networks.

Of course, the perennial school landmine is peer pressure. Across each generation this remains constant. The desire to fit in and be liked is basic to our human nature, but it reaches its pinnacle during the teenage years.

These and other landmines in the school environment are why I want to help parents and teens navigate the teenage years. While the five principles I offer are geared toward school, you will see that they are transferable to other situations you face as a parent. You can help your teenager not just *survive* but actually *thrive*.

Tough Job—Right Approach

Tough jobs can be made more manageable by the right approach. Parents, by the way they lead, react and respond, can either strengthen or weaken their relationship with their child. It all depends on your approach.

"Life coaching" is an increasingly popular term these days. It's a good concept that can be adapted to many areas of life. I believe it also accurately describes the kind of mental positioning a parent needs to have to work with a teen. As you read through the next chapters, you will find tangible suggestions on using the life coaching approach with your teenagers.

A Word to Dads

At various points throughout the book, I'll be offering particular ideas for dads. These ideas are not just for married fathers; divorced dads are encouraged to read along as well. Countless studies from all segments of our culture confirm that the way the dad is involved with his children strongly influences both good and bad outcomes. My own ministry and personal experience have shown me the importance of the father's role. So guys, get ready for some in-your-face observations.

2 **Learning to Life Coach**

Adam and Alex are like lots of kids you know.

They're both sixteen. They come from similar family backgrounds and economic environments. But they behave very differently.

Adam is pretty much a normal teenager. He's not perfect but he generally has respect for his parents and never steps too far out of line. Alex is a different story. There is an underlying anger in his spirit, and he has a constant chip on his shoulder. Alex and his parents are always at each other's throats. Unless something changes, he is headed for trouble.

Adam and Alex are representative of hundreds of young people I've encountered through Youth for Christ. I have learned that bad behavior cannot always be laid at the feet of the parents. Often there are many factors, some unavoidable, that contribute to the way a teen acts.

Generally, however, parents are the one constant in a teenager's development. Studies today confirm that parents are still the biggest influence on their children. The way a parent handles a teenager is often the key to how the teen handles issues. In this particular case, I know that the approach of Adam's parents was markedly different than those of Alex. Adam's parents were interested in Adam's life and activities. Alex's parents were buried in their own worlds of success. Adam's mom and dad treated him like an emerging adult; Alex felt like an afterthought and an inconvenience.

Several years ago the book *The One Minute Manager* became popular in the business community. It was followed by *Leadership and the One Minute Manager.* The primary author, Ken Blanchard, suggested that there are four basic styles of management. A manager manages differently depending on the employee's skills and level of experience.

For example, a new employee has a high level of commitment. They want to do well on their job! But they may have low competence. They've got a lot to learn about their new job. In this situation, you have to manage from a more direct approach. The employee needs structure, control and supervision.

Management Models for Parenting

Child's Development	Parenting Style
Ages 0-11	**Directing** Give structure and control
Ages 12-17	**Coaching** Direct and support
Ages 18-21	**Supporting** Praise, listen and counsel
Ages 22-up	**Delegating** Turn over responsibility for day-to-day decision making

As an employee develops, however, your management style changes. The more competent an employee becomes, the less control you have to exert. In fact, you become less directive and more like a supportive coach. You talk through problems they are experiencing. You help them learn how to take the next step. You offer encouragement.

Good managers are all about helping the employee be successful. In order to do that effectively their management styles will vary.

Even though Blanchard's work has to do with managers and employees, the basic concept is transferable to parents and children. My Christian faith tells me that God gave us children and our job is to help them be successful in life. My experience tells me that parents, like good managers, have to adjust their styles. The chart on page 20 adapts Blanchard's concept as it might relate to parenting.

While styles will vary depending on children's circumstances and personalities, generally parents should think of themselves as a coach for their teenager. Younger children need a strong, directive approach. Like a new employee in the business world, they have high commitment. They're excited about life. But they have little competence. Not only that, they actually *want* you to be directive.

But then "teenagerism" hits! They don't want to be seen with you at the mall. All of a sudden you, the parent, know nothing! Your "sweet little thing" starts to talk back. They question your commands. You—feeling a little threatened—wonder if you should reestablish your position and authority. You're tempted to tighten the screws.

If there is one bit of advice that I could give from my own experience in dealing with the teenage years, it would be this: look for ways to start turning your teenager loose. I know it may feel counterintuitive at this point, but don't let the fact that they are starting to push back force you into a "lock-down" mode. It requires balance and wisdom. You, of course, have to keep the guidelines clear, but look for ways to let them learn responsibility. Put them in charge of keeping the family car clean. Let them paint their own room. (You don't have to live in it, you know.) Find things they want to do, and give them your blessing. Remember, though, that letting them spread their wings now assumes, however, that you did a decent job of being directive when they were younger.

Turning your teenager loose is scary but necessary if you ever want to get them to be responsible for their life decisions. But it requires a good coach.

We can all probably recall examples of bad coaching we've experienced or observed. What are the differences between good coaches and bad coaches? Here are three key characteristics of a good coach.

#1: GOOD COACHES HAVE THE RIGHT MOTIVATION

Two coaches stand out in my not-so-famous basketball career. The first was my sophomore coach in high school and the second coached the varsity team.

My sophomore coach had an attitude. It was obvious, even to this little tenth-grader, that his job was more about his success than mine. It took him a while to learn my name. He often talked down to me and yelled his comments. He never offered a compliment unless it somehow reflected back on his "great coaching ability." In short, my budding basketball career took a nosedive because my motivation factor was constantly being diminished.

My varsity coach was the opposite. I didn't think I'd ever recover from my sophomore experience but this new coach helped me to get back on track. He was calm. He took time to help me personally. He was an encourager. I think I could sum it all up in the statement, "I felt like he was about my success." I was no threat to Michael Jordan, but I did end up contributing to a state basketball championship team.

As your child enters the teenage journey, they need to know—and *feel*—that you are about their success. And that requires self-examination, not by the "coachee," but by the coach.

Often I have seen parents who are less interested in the welfare of their children and more interested in how their children reflect on their reputations as parents. You can hear it when a teenager's parent says something like, "You did what? Don't you understand how that will make us look to our friends?"

Throughout this book I will offer some **Coaching Questions** and **Coaching Exercises**. They are designed to help you examine your own issues and coaching style. Here's the first one.

COACHING QUESTION
In what situations with my teenager do I get defensive about my own reputation?

#2: Good Coaches Create an Open Environment

I didn't realize it until years later, but one of the differences between my two basketball coaches had to do with environment. I'm not talking about the layout of the gym or whether we played inside or outside. (My coach said I had a great outside shot, but unfortunately we played all our games inside.) I'm talking about the atmosphere in which they conducted their work. Was it an open or closed environment?

The environment created by my sophomore coach felt closed. You couldn't talk openly without being criticized. You were afraid to ask a question because you were made to feel dumb. It was not uncommon to be publicly humiliated in front of the crowd for normal mistakes.

Because the motivation of my varsity coach was different, he created a much different environment. I felt welcomed.

My opinions were valuable. My personhood was affirmed. I could be honest. After all, he was about my success.

Moms and dads, you control the environment. It is your job. Not your teenager's. This may be seem strong but I believe it is true. The actions or attitudes of your teen may try to affect the environment, but even then you can set the tone by the way you choose to respond.

Hey, Dads!

Let's face it, we men like to be in control. But a controlling coach can be very intimidating. While I sometimes like to use my positional authority ("Hey, I'm in charge here!") I've realized over the years that the way I speak can either open or close the environment. That doesn't mean you back down from what you want to say. It means that you're more careful about your tone and words.

One of the best discussions of this characteristic is in Gary Smalley's book *The Key to Your Child's Heart* (Word, 1984). He gives very practical suggestions on how to create what he calls an "open spirit" with your children.

Look at the following examples from your teenager's perspective, and ask yourself, *Does this action open or close my teenager's spirit?*

- not saying thank you to your teenagers

- asking their advice on an issue

- affirming their choices

- judging their motives

- being insensitive to their world

- sympathizing with them in a disappointment

- inviting—not commanding—them to go someplace with you

- proudly introducing them to your most important friends

- both parents arguing in front of them

- making sarcastic remarks about their friends

 COACHING QUESTION
What kind of environment do you think you have created for your teenager? Use the following scale.

1	2	3	4	5
CLOSED				OPEN

Now ask your teenager to rate the environment. (Note: if you feel that your teenager can't be honest in his or her answer then you already have a commentary on the environment.)

ANOTHER COACHING QUESTION
Does your teenager come to you for advice? If not, they may be afraid of your response. Regardless of your intentions, they may feel that you talk down to them or discount the value of their question. Such feelings close their spirit.

#3: GOOD COACHES LOOK FOR WHAT'S AHEAD

John Wooden is college basketball's most famous and successful coach. He certainly had the players' best interest at heart. Even today, twenty years after his coaching ended and over the age of ninety, he keeps in contact with hundreds of his players.

Because he had the right motivation, he created an open environment. This didn't mean he didn't have rules. Players absolutely knew the boundaries, and that contributed to the open atmosphere because everyone was on the same page. They also knew they would be treated with fairness. There were no favorites for whom the rules could be bent.

John Wooden also possessed something intrinsic to great coaches—he was always ahead of the game. Whether in an actual game or looking at the game as a whole, Wooden thought "further out." Good coaches are good anticipators both in the game and conceptually. They strive to know what's coming next so they can be prepared.

As a parent, something you have is experience, both good and bad. Use it! It is easy to get all wrapped up in today's issues but you need to look at what might be ahead for your teenager and help them be prepared. Even though your teen is an emerging adult, they still tend to make decisions based on immediate rather than long-term consequences.

While the first two characteristics have to do with attitude, the last characteristic requires potentially becoming a little more intrusive into your teenager's life. Your teen's acceptance of your "intrusiveness" will depend on how you have practiced the first two characteristics. If your teenager is constantly unresponsive, go back and evaluate your motivation and the environment you've created.

 COACHING QUESTION
What long-term issues are you afraid to discuss with your teenager knowing they will feel you're too intrusive? Is there something you have done or not done in the past that contributes to this blockage?

Good coaching is simply a way to describe the successful parenting relationship. If you want your teen to have a healthy, supportive experience, live out these vital characteristics of life coaching.

3

LifeCoach Principle #1

HELP YOUR TEEN IDENTIFY GOALS

Winnie the Pooh was right:

"If you don't know where you are going, how will you know when you get there?" Life with no goals—nothing to shoot for, no place to go—gets you nowhere.

I've seen it so often in the kids with whom I've worked. Teenagers who just wait for things to come to them can survive. But young people like Larry begin to thrive because they set their sights on something they want to accomplish.

Larry was not a gifted athlete, but he was a gifted musician. He wasn't sure where his skill would lead him, but he was diligent at developing his skills. Somehow, someway, his goal was to perform. His parents offered encouragement and support, costing them their money and time.

But today, Larry's parents would tell you it was all worth

it as they watch their son perform on Broadway in a major role in *Phantom of the Opera*. Larry openly acknowledges God's hand in all this but credits his supportive parents for helping establish and support his dream.

Goals are valuable tools in life. Unless you understand the value of a tool, you'll probably never experience its benefits. For a long time I didn't understand the real value of computers. I now know that I missed out on a tremendous tool that could help my life in so many ways. So it is with goals.

Goals are critical to success in every area of life. Coaches, bosses, politicians and teach-

A goal is simply something you want to accomplish.

ers depend on them. Businesses, governments, teams and companies use them to provide direction. Circumstances, crises and time may require changing one's goals. But written, spoken or unconscious objectives work to shape a person's behaviors, attitudes and life.

Your teenager needs to learn about goals and their importance. Here's some valuable rationale:

• Goals provide the compass and map for a person's future.

• Goals give structure to dreams and a blueprint for accomplishment.

- Goals give purpose to life and add value to time.

- Goals and their accomplishment provide a reason for celebration.

- Goals help you feel good about yourself.

Here's a coaching exercise that you could use with your teenager to discuss the value of creating goals.

COACHING EXERCISE
Discuss the following with your teenager:

> • *What would a team be like without goals?*
> • *When I achieve a goal I feel . . .*
> • *Not having goals would mean . . .*
> • *Making goals is hard because . . .*
> • *When I don't have goals, it makes me feel . . .*

Selecting the Right Goals

Beginning the conversation about goals at school with your teenager can be threatening for both of you. But remember the good coaching characteristic that good coaches create an open environment. If your teen feels that you're about his or her success, then continue by creating a supportive conversational atmosphere. Goal setting is not about right or wrong—it's about identifying the passions of your heart. As a parent, you may want to set some goals yourself so that each of you can talk about how you are progressing.

The most difficult part of goal setting for most of us is prioritizing all that we want to accomplish. This problem with teenagers is amplified because they often want to do "everything." So how do you help your teenager center in on three or four goals to accomplish in their school year?

Begin by writing down all the possibilities of goals. The list may contain items like

- improving my grades
- making the basketball team
- getting a date with _____
- getting a job
- buying a car
- serving on student government
- playing a solo in band
- making the debate team

The next step is *prioritizing*. Here's a great tool to help. It's called a tournament bracket. Coaches from every sport are familiar with it. It's a device to show how teams eliminate one another in order to get down to the final two teams. In a college basketball tournament it may look like this:

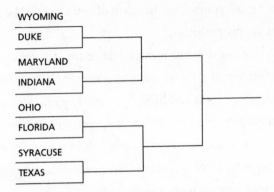

If Wyoming beats Duke in the first round (fat chance, and I'm from Wyoming), they move on in the tournament. The game bracket continues until two teams are left and they would play for the championship.

Let's adapt this model and put the eight potential goals above in the brackets. It could look like this:

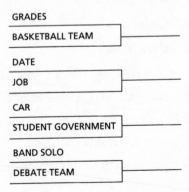

Now the hard part. Your teenager, and you too if you're also setting goals, has to decide which potential goal is more valuable. Is making the basketball team more important than making the debate team? The choices are still difficult because all the potential goals have value, but this exercise will force you into making decisions.

Your decision-making process can be enhanced through the counsel of others and examining whether your giftedness matches your goals. From a spiritual perspective, you can evaluate your goals through a grid that includes prayer and reflection on what God might have for you. If you believe, as I do, that God has created you with unique gifts and wants to use those gifts for his glory, then those beliefs will obviously influence your decisions.

Using the tournament bracket and the counsel of others, examining your own giftedness, and following your spiritual values will give you a great head start on making the best choices.

(Coaching hint: This exercise will lead to some great discussions where you will be able to use another characteristic of a good coach: looking for what's ahead. Help your teenagers think through what goal will have the greatest long-range benefit.)

Their Goals or Yours?

As you make your choices, be aware that you may be tempted to impose your goals on your teenagers. My brother-in-law Dan struggled with this temptation.

Dan and my sister-in-law live in a very small Midwestern town, population three hundred. Sports, especially high school sports, are the major unifying factor in their community. The town's parents want to see their kids do well on the sports teams.

Dan's older twin sons realized this dream. They both were great athletes, making varsity teams in basketball and track. But things were different with the third son, Gareth. It soon became evident that Gareth didn't have the natural talent or desire to pursue sports like his older brothers.

This was difficult for Dan. His goal for Gareth was to see him do well in sports. Dan kept giving Gareth opportunities to make progress, but Dan was disappointed by Gareth's lack of athletic success. In addition, Gareth's talents and interests were in very different areas. He was good at music. He was sensitive and caring toward people. He leaned more toward the arts than athletics.

Fortunately, over time Dan began to see his third son's areas of strength. Once he gave Gareth opportunities to develop his natural talents, Gareth began to shine and thrive in his own fields. Today, Gareth is a youth pastor and married. His music is an important part of his ministry. The kids love him. He has a great heart. Dan let his son discover and express his own talents before Dan's sports goals could create resentment and rebellion in Gareth's life.

COACHING QUESTION
In what ways might you be tempted to impose one or more of your goals on your teenager?

MAKING GOALS REACHABLE

Perhaps the greatest deterrent to goal achievement is making unreachable goals in the first place. Here are some suggestions for setting goals that will increase a teenager's potential for reaching them.

Goals need to be realistic. To encourage your teen in realistic goal setting, know your teenager's capacities but balance your knowledge with realistic encouragement. If your teens don't have the skill or capacity to make the team or get an A in algebra, they'll only be frustrated if they set and try to reach unrealistic goals. They can't expect to make first chair in band if they've only been playing their instrument for six months. They'll probably never play center on the high school basketball team if they're only 5'6". While it is important that you teach your children to "think and dream big," also help them keep an accurate "dream-balance." Goals that aren't realistic set up potential disappointments. *Goals need to be big enough to matter, small enough to reach and strong enough to build on.*

Goals need to be specific. If goals aren't specific, they can't be measured. If goals can't be measured, then a person will never know how she or he did. If your teen says, "I want to make the football team this year," that goal can be measured. It will be easy to tell if the goal is met or not. But if your teenager says, "I'd like to be a better student," that's too vague. How do you define what being a "better student" means? A specific academic goal would be to say, "I want to raise my GPA from 3.1 to 3.6." *Goals that aren't specific and measurable only lead young people to feel mediocre and dissatisfied.*

Goals are met in stages. Only superheroes like Superman can leap tall buildings in a single bound. The rest of the human race climbs the stairs of accomplishment one at a time. Having big goals is important, but teenagers need help to understand how goals build in sequence. Barry Bonds became a home run king one home run at a time.

Set smaller, intermediate goals on the way to accomplishing bigger goals. *Just like saving for a car, goals require ongoing investments for the future.*

Goals need to be flexible. I've learned to write my schedule and goals in pencil. Why? Because I realized that life is full of interruptions and detours. People who end up accomplishing their objectives do so because they've learned how to adjust to life's interruptions and detours. Walt Disney went bankrupt five times and faced what appeared to be insurmountable obstacles on the way to building Disneyland. Disney succeeded because *he knew how to move in another direction when one road was blocked.*

Goals should reflect values and principles. As coaching parents, we want our children to learn and live out our values. The goals a person pursues reflect what's important to him or her. The culture around them tells our teenagers what to think, do, be and buy. These relentless messages create great confusion in the minds and decision-making capabilities of this generation of teenagers. In a recent survey, over 50 percent of teens said that they don't know the difference between what's right and what's wrong.

Often in my Youth for Christ experience I've encountered young people who've spent time pursuing goals like being the best dressed, most popular or a sports star, only to find out that their accomplishments brought them no inner satisfaction. As you discuss your teenager's goals, bring up the value question.

COACHING EXERCISE
Ask the "why questions." When you're talking with your teenager about goals, it's a great and appropriate time to ask "why questions" like "Why do you want to have a better GPA?" and "Why do you want this particular job?" Of course, you need to be careful here, because a "why" question can seem accusatory, as if by your very asking you're saying what they want is wrong. Make sure your teen knows that your motive in asking is to help them identify the values they're using to shape their goals.

AVOIDING PITFALLS

In working toward their goals, certain "pitfalls" can cause teenagers to stumble.

The performance-based pitfall. Avoiding this pitfall is perhaps one of the most delicate balancing acts for the parent-coach. On the one hand, we want to encourage our teens to do all they can to reach their goals. On the other hand, we should be careful not to put too much emphasis on "outcomes."

The key? Always reinforce that your teenager is valu-able not because she or he accomplished a goal but because they're created uniquely, with a unique personality and set of skills. Let them know that you love them and are proud of them whether they meet goals or not. Affirm them with comments like

- "I love the determination you showed in your effort."
- "I see a new skill developing in you."
- "Thank you for going after this. It says a lot about your character."

The unspoken goal pitfall. You need to be aware that your teenager may have "unspoken" goals for the school year. Maybe they haven't mentioned these goals to you, though they may have been discussed quite openly with their peers. And that peer involvement can be both positive and negative.

The danger in unspoken goals is that teenagers may be pressured to compromise their belief system in order to gain something that could cause long-term damage and emotional wounding to their soul. An unspoken goal may not be bad in itself but can become negative by the amount of energy or compromise used to accomplish it.

Some examples of unspoken goals would be

- getting a date with a particular person
- achieving popularity

- wanting fame or recognition
- "just trying" drugs or alcohol
- wanting to be a part of a particular group

These kinds of potential unspoken goals are why it is important that you monitor your teen's schedule, activities, friends and their friends' families. Meet their friends. Invite the kids to hang out at your house. Many parents have learned to welcome the "inconvenience" of having teenagers gather at their home. That way, parents can keep a finger on the pulse of what their kids are thinking, how they're feeling and what's going on between them and their friends.

Hey, Dads!

Don't leave this up to the mother! Of course she participates, but all too often it all falls on her shoulders. Learn to engage your teenagers. Meet their friends. They may even like you!

The "I've tried this before" pitfall. This is a common response parents get from teenagers who have set goals before and then not been satisfied with the outcomes. In most cases, this disappointment results from the teen having not established realistic goals in the first place.

Perhaps when the teenager worked toward the goal, she or he "failed" because no one coached, encouraged and supported her or his efforts. In this case, rather than risk embarrassment from failure, the teen refuses to try again.

Helping your teenager escape this pitfall is like teaching them to reactivate a stick-shift car when it's stalled. You have to sit next to them and patiently let them gain confidence while they learn the feel of the gas and gears. It takes a while to "smooth out the clutch," but confidence and speed can only come with practice.

I confess that, living in Denver, I'm a big Broncos football fan. I moved to Denver the year they traded for John Elway. It was exciting—and painful. As fans, we had to endure Elway's erratic passing, his poor decision making, his propensity to try to win the game himself, and his inexperience at reading defenses. I wish I could show you some of the negative articles written about him in the early part of his career. But flashes of brilliance generated hope. We hung on—and John delivered, because he refused to give in to these pitfalls, and because his coach, Dan Reeves, wouldn't let him use his pitfalls as an excuse.

COACHING EXERCISE
Tell your teenager about a time when you pursued a goal only to discover that it was a bust or that achieving it wasn't what you really wanted.

Spending time developing goals is another part of the tough job of parenting, but it can be very rewarding and many life lessons can be discussed during the process. When done correctly, establishing goals will help your teenager move from just surviving to thriving.

4

LifeCoach Principle #2

SHOW YOUR TEEN HOW TO FIND BALANCE IN LIFE

It's one thing to have goals.

It's another thing to know how to reach them.

When I was doing direct campus ministry, one of my high schools had a great swimming team. They were a reflection of a great coach. He was good at setting goals but even better at developing the strategy that eventually accomplished many of the goals.

One of his secrets was helping his individual swimmers discipline their own lives. He knew that disciplined swimmers produce disciplined teams. Disciplined teams have a better chance of meeting their goals. The coach knew and taught that a big part of personal discipline is learning how to prioritize and balance the different areas of your life.

As you coach your teenager for school and life, helping

her or him learn the disciplines of prioritization and balance is critical for personal growth and goal achievement.

DAILY PLANNERS AND PDAS

As parents, we know how busy life can be. Imagine trying to juggle all the duties and functions of life without experience or emotional maturity. That's where many of our kids are today. A very complex life has been thrust upon them without supplying the necessary tools to cope.

This millennial generation started carrying daily planners to schedule concert dates and soccer practices, and to mark which weekends they'd spend with which parent. Their schedules have become overloaded, and they are confronted with options that multiply faster than rabbits on steroids. Now they have increasingly sophisticated personal digital assistants to help them stay afloat.

Multitasking is more natural and necessary for today's teenagers. Studying often involves simultaneously reading a book while instant messaging online, watching TV, listening to a CD and talking on a cell phone. To adults this may seem overwhelming, but to today's teenager it's considered normal. All of us are blessed and cursed by this information age. Today we have more media channels, restaurants, shops, activities and information than ever before, but how do we know "who's on first" and "what's coming next?" Simple. We just need more time! Unfortunately, that just doesn't happen.

One of my favorite stories illustrates the dilemma. A man had a conversation with God. The man asked, "God, what is a thousand years like to you?"

"Like a second," God replied.

After a slight pause the man asked. "What is a million dollars like to you?"

"Probably like a penny," God responded.

Thinking he had God just where he wanted him, the man asked one more question. "Well, God, can you give me a penny?"

"Sure," said God. "Just a second."

We may wish that we could see time from God's perspective, but we can't. Time equalizes all humans. Bill Gates has no more time than my grandmother. So having more time is not really the answer. The answer is knowing how to use your time effectively. Learning how to prioritize and balance a schedule is key to your teenager using time wisely.

COACHING QUESTION
If asked, could you tell your teenager your priorities?

WHERE DO WE START?

Once goals have been established, your teenager needs to identify the activities necessary to help accomplish those goals. Try the following exercise to help your son or daughter identify the activities that might help meet the goal.

Make a list. Let's say your teenager has a goal of making first chair in the band. Have your teen make a list of the kind of activities that may need to take place in order for this goal to be accomplished. The list may include

- taking private lessons
- buying a better instrument
- increasing practice time
- meeting with the band director
- listening to performances by accomplished musicians

Making lists can help free the brain and help your teenager focus on the most important activities. But remember, this exercise should be performed for each of your goals. Your teenager may want to use a computer spreadsheet or organizational software for this process; no matter how it's done, in the end the list could be long and overwhelming.

Prioritize. The next step is to determine what has to be done and what doesn't have to be done. This is where we want to scream, "Just give me more time!" Prioritiza-

tion is hard work and sometimes frustrating. Let me offer
two questions that may help.

The first question: "Is this activity important or just urgent?" Stephen Covey has done a great job helping us see
the difference between the two in his book *The Seven Habits
of Highly Effective People*. His son Sean offers some practical
exercises toward this end in his book *The Seven Habits of
Highly Effective Teens*.

Your teenager may feel the urgency to go visit a particular friend ("Mom, they need me"). In light of their musical goal, however, they may need to practice their instrument. Visiting their friend may feel more urgent, but is it
more important? Prioritizing life is about deciding what is
really important in the long run, not just urgent right now.
Of course, there is no general formula for this because all
situations differ, but asking the question makes you think.
And don't forget, sometimes something can be both important *and* urgent.

The second question is a variation on the first: "Am I
going to be effective or just efficient?" A teenager may load
their schedule with all kinds of activities. Because they're
busy, they think they're accomplishing their goal. But is
this the *best* use of their time? In the first question you ask,
"What is important?" In the second you ask, "Am I being

effective?" Both questions are designed to help your teenager weigh issues carefully so he or she can emerge with the best priorities.

BALANCE

We live in a culture that values getting tasks and whole jobs done. That's even reflected here on my emphasis on goal accomplishment. That in itself is not bad. Even Jesus emphasized this value in John 15:8 when he said, "This is to my Father's glory, that you bear much fruit, showing yourselves to be my disciples." Bearing fruit is about accomplishment.

Hey, Dads!

I've got two zingers for you now.

1. We're famous for giving good advice but not following it ourselves. Here's a great opportunity for you to create an open environment by sharing your schedule and how you manage it. Talk about the difficulties of sometimes having to choose between better and best.

2. You'll probably agree that spending time with your teenager is both important and effective. Here's the test. Is time with your teenager on your "to do" list? (I warned you that this could get personal!)

But we are called human *be*-ings, not human *do*-ings. Teens need to understand that goal accomplishment, in itself, can be empty, tiring and unfulfilling unless their schedule also reflects time for what I call "The Big Easys": rest, personal growth, play time and relationship building.

Rest. Within a teenager's DNA is the desire to do *everything*. Part of growing up for teens and college students is discovering and pushing their bodies to the limit. Since they have superabundance of natural energy, they often don't realize that they're running on mere adrenaline, junk food or Starbucks. They spend more time with peers, at work and with media activities than they do getting enough rest. Surveys show that when teenagers have too many priorities, sleep is what suffers most. Researchers have proven that regular sleep patterns help a person in all areas of their life. But adolescents' bodies need a lot of rest and without it their school performance will suffer. As a life coach you have to sometimes get in their face and make sure rest is a part of their schedule.

Personal growth. Priorities and schedules need to reflect emphasis and time for personal development. If spiritual life is important to teens, they'll need time to develop it. They'll want to make sure that their schedule incorporates time for fellowship, Bible study, prayer and other spiritual activities. Or maybe they'll want to improve their art skills so they take an art class at the junior college on Saturday mornings.

This kind of growth must be personalized, but as a life coach you should look for ways to encourage this in your teens. They won't reach their best without developing themselves as a whole person.

Play time. We all need it. It's a time to let your mind relax and change your perspective. For some, it may be golf. For others, it may be reading a novel. Still others may want to take a long run or go to a movie.

It's also okay for your teenager just to "veg out." Now you may be saying, "Hey, my kid has that one nailed." I understand. I'm pretty good at this one myself. But often I find two problems. First, I can feel guilty—or you may make your teenager feel guilty. If you actually put "veg time" in your schedule, it helps eliminate the guilt. You've declared it to be important and effective.

Hey, Dads!

The way you handle this issue in our own life will have great impact on your child. Do you practice The Big Easys? If not, you don't have to say anything. Your teenager will already know it.

Second, often vegging out is reactive rather than proactive. In other words, people end up vegging out because they're burned out. By proactively putting some veg time in your schedule, you're helping to eliminate burnout.

COACHING EXERCISE
Let's say your teenager likes to read science fiction novels. Buy one and give it to them with a note encouraging them to take time to read it. Let them know that you know that time spent like this is important.

Relationship building. Our friendships are a huge part of "being" in life. A balanced approach to life provides opportunities for relationships to develop and grow.

Wise coaches understand the part "chemistry" plays on a team. Sometimes very talented players don't win championships because the chemistry is wrong. There's too much infighting. On the other hand, some teams can succeed because the chemistry working together is so powerful that it makes up for lesser talent. The right relationships can be the chemistry that will motivate your teenager toward goal accomplishment.

Helping establish priorities and balance in your teenager's life is often like establishing goals—they need to be done with an eraser in hand. Situations will change.

New priorities will emerge that you didn't expect. Sometimes your teenager may need an extra amount of rest. The operative word for good coaches is flexibility. Your willingness to adapt can open or close the spirit of your teenager.

 COACHING QUESTION
How would you rate your "flexibility"?

1	2	3	4	5
VERY FLEXIBLE				**VERY RIGID**

This too requires experience and wisdom. I'm not suggesting you give in on every issue, but my experience—both personally and professionally—suggests that parents err on the side of being too rigid, thinking they have to control the situation that way rather than rationally deciding whether being flexible might be the best course of action for all concerned.

 COACHING ASSESSMENT
Consider the following situation.

Your daughter has a test at 9:00 a.m. in her French class. She wants to get an A in this class, and she'll need to do well on this test to accomplish this goal. Unfortunately, she has been up most of the night with the stomach flu. What do you do: call the teacher and see if she can take the test later? Let her sleep in and hope the teacher understands? Get her to class on time and hope for the best?

This is real life, isn't it? Each parent, depending on your personality and the personality of your teenager, will have to determine how flexible you are. There often is no right or wrong answer in such situations—only choices. My point is that a parent must be willing to be flexible. That will then free you up to make the best choice.

5 LifeCoach Principle #3
TEACH YOUR TEEN TO FAIL FORWARD

Goals are important.

Knowing how to prioritize and balance those goals is key to their accomplishment. But what happens when things don't go the way you planned? The next step in our process of learning how to thrive often separates those who succeed from those who don't.

In his twenties, a man failed twice in business, lost and won a state senate race and had a nervous breakdown. In his thirties, he lost a bid for Congress, then won, then lost the seat he'd won. His forties brought defeat twice for the U.S. Senate and once for vice president. This wasn't what this man had planned.

But at the age of fifty-one, Abraham Lincoln was elected to the highest office in the land and became one of our greatest presidents. Lincoln knew how to fail forward. He learned how to take the emotion of disappointment and turn it into the energy of success. This principle helped Abraham Lincoln become a "thriver."

We all face failure. Walt Disney is credited with saying that life is 70 percent failure. Having goals means you will have disappointments. How you deal with those disappointments is key.

In a microwave world of instant gratification it's often difficult for young people to recognize and accept how much time, training and effort is required for success. It's important for them to learn that whenever they set and attempt to achieve goals, *they will meet resistance.* It may come in the form of people, individual limitations or external circumstances, but no matter how it comes, it *will* come. But the people who end up accomplishing their goals are the people who've learned how to overcome the resistance they face.

FAILING FORWARD IS ABOUT PROGRESS

Failing is a bad word in our culture. No one wants to be known as a failure. Certainly your teenager is not looking for that title.

But let me suggest that good coaching is about helping your teen think differently about failing. If approached correctly, failing can actually be a good thing. Failing means you've tried. That's good. And when you learn something from your failures, that's even better.

Imagine the great, modern-day home run hitter Barry Bonds striking out, as he often did. On the way back to the dugout he tells himself, "I've failed. I'm never going to bat again because I don't want to be embarrassed." That may sound a little silly, but I'll guarantee you that every good hitter has thought about some variation of that statement.

However, Bonds and other great hitters agree with Wayne Gretzky, the great hockey player, who said, "I miss 100 percent of the shots I don't take." For Bonds, he has to be up at bat to hit a home run.

Just as important as being at the plate is what Bonds does after he strikes out. While sitting on the bench, he's thinking about what he did wrong. He's analyzing the pitcher and thinking about his own swing. He may even ask the Giants's hitting instructor if he has any observations. He's trying to learn from the strikeout.

Your teenager will fail. Life coaches understand that failure creates a teachable moment. Let your teen experience the emotion of the moment but don't let them dwell there. Capture the moment to look ahead and create progress. One of the quickest ways to dispel the sadness of failure is to create hope for the future.

And remember, the longer you sit on the bench thinking about your strikeout, the bigger failure looks. You need to get up to bat again as quickly as possible. When your teenager "fails," give them another opportunity, as soon as possible, to succeed at something else.

FAILING FORWARD IS ABOUT PERSPECTIVE

As a life coach, you have the advantage of life experience on your side. You know that an Olympic athlete doesn't win a gold medal on the first try. An artist doesn't produce a masterpiece with the first canvas. First attempts are normally just that—attempts.

You also see failure from a different perspective. Teenagers have a smaller frame of reference than adults. We adults have had thousands of experiences over several decades of life. Teenagers have had a lot fewer experiences in a lot less time. So one failure can look very big to them. We see things differently.

Our work in Youth for Christ is about helping young people see life from God's viewpoint. Before you can trust God, you often need to understand his character and how he operates. We use the following story to illustrate a central biblical truth about God—he can turn apparent failure into something good.

Once there was an old man who, although poor, was envied by his village, for he owned a beautiful horse.

One morning the horse was not in the stable. All the village came to see him. "You old fool," they scoffed. "You could have gotten any price you wanted for that horse. You've been cursed with misfortune."

The old man spoke. "The horse is gone. Whether it be a curse or a blessing, I can't say. All we can see is a fragment. Who can say what will come next?"

After fifteen days, the horse returned, bringing a dozen wild horses with him. Once again the people gathered. "Old man, you were right. What we thought was a curse was a blessing."

He responded, "I can only say that the horse is back and a dozen horses returned with him. We dare not judge if it is a blessing or not."

The old man's only son began to break the wild horses. He fell and broke both legs.

The villagers said to the old man, "The dozen horses were not a blessing. Your only son has broken legs, and now you have no one to help you. You are poorer than ever."

The old man spoke. "You people seem obsessed with judging. My son broke his legs. Who knows if it is a blessing or a curse?"

A few weeks later the country went to war. All the young men of the village were required to join the army. Only the injured young man was exempt.

The people came crying and screaming. "Your son's accident was a blessing! His legs may be broken, but they will mend. At least he is with you. Our sons are gone forever!"

The old man spoke again. "No one knows. It does not profit to call anything a blessing or a curse, for God is at work in everything for good to those who are called according to his purpose."

Even if you don't share my Christian faith, the story still illustrates a truism of life: it comes in fragments. As a life coach, you can help your teen see that an apparent failure is not the end of the world.

COACHING EXERCISE
Be prepared to share a story from your own life that demonstrates how an apparent failure really worked for good in your life.

FAILING FORWARD IS ABOUT PERSISTENCE

On October 29, 1941, Winston Churchill gave a speech in which he exhorted his audience to persevere during the trials of World War II. He said, "Never give in. Never give in. Never, never, never, never—in nothing, great or small, large or petty—never give in, except to convictions of honour and good sense." What a life lesson for a life coach to impart to their teenager!

Your teen has grown up in a world of the immediate. Complex problems are resolved in a thirty-minute TV show. People become rich with the purchase of a single lottery ticket. Compare that to the children of previous generations who worked on family farms. There was no immediate crop. Sometimes it took up to a year to see the results they wanted.

Often our kids give up early because they haven't been taught or experienced the value of "hanging in there." As a life coach you can help motivate your teenager to greater persistence not only by talking about the value of it but by your attitude. They need to *feel* your support, encouragement and belief in them.

COACHING QUESTION
What do you do in your life that demonstrates persistence to your teenager?

FAILING FORWARD ROADBLOCKS

Teenagers face some common problems when learning how to fail forward. Here are just three.

The "comparison" roadblock. All of us are guilty of comparing ourselves to others, but this is a particularly big temptation for teenagers. A part of learning to fail forward is learning about your giftedness. You can't do everything. You don't have all the skills. Life coaching means helping your teen discover, often through disappointment, what they're good at. That comes from trying, maybe failing, making adjustments and trying again. Learning what you're good at only comes through persistence.

The "mind game" roadblock. Failure is not so much about what happens on the field as what happens in your head. Perhaps the single most important ingredient in learning to fail forward is attitude. That happens in your mind. Attitude is determined by your belief system. If your teenager believes that failing forward is about progress rather than defeat, they'll have a more positive attitude. If they believe that "bad stuff" can be turned into "good stuff," that makes a whale of a difference in your approach.

The "poor me" roadblock. Disappointment and failure can be excused by a "victim mentality." It's easier some-

times to just feel sorry for yourself rather than to persevere. And a life coach needs great wisdom to tell the difference between needing to encourage persistence and
actually needing to rescue.

Hey, Dads!

The tendency for mom is often to rescue. The tendency
for dad is often to say, "Suck it up." Just be careful that
you don't always go with your tendency. Ask for a fe-
male perspective, weigh it carefully and then make
your judgment. Remember: your teenager's attitude is
at stake.

Most successful athletes point to a coach that was key
in their life. Successful businesspersons will point to a
teacher or mentor. I'll guarantee you that successful
coaches, teachers and mentors taught their students how
to fail forward.

6

LifeCoach Principle #4

HELP YOUR TEEN COPE WITH ANGER

If your teenager exhibits anger, you're not alone.

This generation of young people has a lot of anger. It can be the result of broken homes, both parents working, no boundaries, too much materialism or just feeling alone. It shows itself in violence, disrespect, attitude or irritability. We see it every day in kids with whom we work.

If you're trying to accomplish something in life—setting goals for school, prioritizing and balancing your schedules, learning to fail forward—you'll probably face anger. It's a natural result of trying to move ahead and dealing with the frustrations and problems that come.

You've seen it in a high school athlete. She wants to be All-State. She has all the talent in the world but instead of controlling her anger, the anger controls her. It affects her play and self-confidence. Unless she learns to manage her anger, she'll never reach her potential.

COPING SKILLS

As a life coach, helping your teenager understand and cope with anger is important, difficult and sometimes threatening. Let me offer some observations that may help you in this delicate process.

> *"In your anger, do not sin":*
> *Do not let the sun go down*
> *while you are still angry.*
> **EPHESIANS 4:26**

Anger is not wrong. Anger is normal. It is an emotion that just happens. Often anger is a secondary emotion. In other words, it is a result of something else that has happened. Frustration and personal hurt are the two biggest culprits. Helping your teen understand this truth will remove the guilt that is often associated with this subject. Be careful about conveying the message to your teenager that they are automatically wrong if they feel anger.

Anger can be destructive. Someone has said that there is only one letter difference between anger and danger. Life coaches help their teenager know that what you do with your anger is the key. Anger expressed in the wrong way can sever relationships, ruin your reputation, generate turmoil and create deeper problems. It can destroy momentum, crush morale and erode potential. If you just let anger simmer, this unresolved emotion can turn into a huge internal garbage dump that oozes emotional toxins and poisonous attitudes.

Here are some suggestions that may help your teen—and you—respond appropriately to anger. They come from *Caring for Your Teenager* by Dr. Donald Greydanus and Philip Bashe.

- When you feel anger, take a five-minute personal time out to think about and defuse your emotions. (Never punish anyone when you're angry.)

- Breathe deeply and relax your muscles.

- Stay calm and speak in a softer voice, even when others around you are yelling.

- Use *I,* and refer to specific, current situations, not generalized terms when you're addressing people with whom you're angry. Say, "*I'm* upset that you didn't clean up after yourself in the kitchen," not "*You* never clean up after yourself and you think I'm your maid."

- If your teenager tires to hook you into an angry conflict, keep your cool and don't take the bait.

- If you have made a mistake and lost your temper, be sure to apologize to your teenager. This will model for them how they can make their own future apologies and learn the freedom to forgive others.

DISCOVER THE SOURCE OF THE ANGER

Remember that anger is normally a secondary emotion. Discovering the source of the anger can help defuse the emotion and manage the response.

Uncovering the source of anger can be as simple as identifying the frustration that comes from being the younger brother to a star athlete. Or it can be as complicated as the deep wounds that may exist from a child feeling abandoned when the parents went through a painful divorce. If your teenager regularly exhibits anger, you can be sure that there is probably something else below the surface. In some cases, you may want to seek professional help to discover the source.

My experience tells me that most teenagers don't like the anger they feel. Most of the time, however, they don't know what to do about it. That's where a life coach can be so helpful. Acknowledge the anger. Don't condemn, and gently begin to examine what caused the emotion to happen in the first place.

COACHING QUESTION

Would your teenager say you handle your anger well?
If not, why not?

CLEAN OUT THE EMOTIONAL CLOSET

There are two aspects to this. First, if you feel like your
teenager is angry, give them the liberty to express it appropriately. Buried emotions are like pushing on a balloon with two hands. There is only so much space for the
air inside, so you create a bulge. Enough pressure will
cause the balloon to rupture.
Teens need to have the freedom to get their anger out.

*Don't let the pain of the
past destroy the thrill
of the present and the joy
of the future.*

Second, see if there are
other emotions buried in the
closet that are not being expressed. When you're trying
to discover the source, you're dealing with expressed anger. When you dig deeper, you're probing for emotions
that your teenager may not even realize exist.

As a life coach you're helping your teen learn emotional
accountability. No one else can be in charge of my emotions. Your teenager needs to learn how to recognize what
may be in the closet and get it out in the open.

COACHING EXERCISE

Use your teenager's closet or your own to illustrate how unresolved emotions can pile up. It can get so bad that you might not even have room for new clothes.

ANGER CAN BE CONSTRUCTIVE

As we've said, anger is simply an emotion. It's an emotion of energy. Your nerves are more alert and your senses are heightened. It taps into your passion. You feel motivated to do something. The secret is to make sure you channel the energy of anger in the right direction.

Our baseball team in Colorado is the Rockies. They're just a little bit better than the Nuggets, our basketball team. But we have a great hitting first baseman named Todd Helton. He's consistently in the running for the batting title. I've learned a lot from him about the constructive side of anger.

Like most hitters, Todd doesn't always agree with the umpire's opinion about balls and strikes. Often I've seen the look on Helton's face when the ump calls what appears to be an outside pitch a strike. Todd backs out of the box, grimaces for a moment, then refocuses. You can almost hear him saying to himself, "Okay, this ump must have only one eye. But forget it. I'm a little ticked now, and I'm going to use this surge of energy I'm feeling to get a hit." Many times I've seen him do just that. Learning to turn the energy of anger into constructive energy is one thing that makes him superior.

There's another good thing about anger. It shows you care. Look at how many wonderful and necessary things have been accomplished in life because someone got angry. Lincoln changed a culture because he was angry about slavery. Reagan helped "tear down the wall" because he was angry that people didn't have freedom. Mothers Against Drunk Drivers have had a wonderful influence because they were angry that drunks were killing their children.

Good life coaches have learned how to turn the energy of anger into something good.

Hey, Dads!

As men, we don't always handle anger the right way. Sometimes we try to control situations with our anger. Sometimes we use it to create fear. It may be time for an honest gut check. If you're falling short you may want to find a friend, a pastor or a professional to help you face your anger issues. Like all these principles, the way you live with your anger speaks louder than your words.

7

LifeCoach Principle #5

COME ALONGSIDE YOUR TEEN

Successful life coaches don't just stay on the sidelines—

they come alongside. This principle will make or break your influence. Coming alongside helps produce "thrivers."

Interestingly enough, today's generation of young people want their parents to be more involved. In a recent survey conducted by the Gallup Institute and reported in *The Seven Cries of Today's Teens*, researcher Timothy Smith says, "Teens want to be supported in what is important to them."

A little object lesson here might help. Picture a megaphone and a towel. The megaphone is often held by a coach on the sidelines shouting instructions to the team. His voice is commanding and the megaphone gives a sense of control and authority.

The towel, on the other hand, represents servanthood. This coach comes alongside and either figuratively or actually experiences what the player is experiencing. This coach may even use the towel to wipe the sweat from the player.

The megaphone is impersonal; it never really touches you. The towel is more about you and what you are experiencing. Towels represent support, encouragement and concern.

COMING ALONGSIDE MEANS ACTIVE LISTENING

Overstated perhaps, but the coach on the sidelines with the megaphone doesn't really care about the opinions of the players. After all, he is the coach. He knows what to do. All a player has to do is respond to his commands.

Life coaches who come alongside want to hear from their teenagers. They're not just there to shout advice and commands. Remember, your teenager is an emerging adult with valid observations, thoughts and opinions. Most of those observations, thoughts and opinions have been heavily influenced by you, so they ought to be worth something!

Listening to your teenager struggle with goals, priorities, failures and anger is best done from a supportive style rather than a directive style. Listen, not just to give advice but to help teens discover their own answers. The more a teenager is empowered to take his or her own actions, the faster he or she will mature and grow.

Above all, listen without judging. Most of the time, your teenager will be talking about how they feel about something. The quickest way to shut down the dialogue is for them to feel judgment from you.

Additional tips for good listening:

- Don't interrupt.
- Give them your *full* attention.
- Look them in the eye.
- Ask if they want your opinion.
- Honor their privacy.

Megaphone coaches *talk*—that's what the megaphone is for. You don't hold the megaphone up to your ear. Towel coaches get close enough to *listen*.

Hey, Dads!

Whether we are handy or not, we guys like to fix stuff— even our kids' problems. But resist getting "to the bottom line." Just listen. No advice. No solution. No "Well, all you have to do is suck it up." And you'd be remarkably surprised how much it would mean to your teenager if they heard you say, "Boy, I'm not sure I have an answer for that. What would you do?"

COMING ALONGSIDE MEANS GIVING ENCOURAGEMENT AND PRAISE

Life coaches need to create an environment where "seldom is heard a discouraging word." Discouraging words motivate no one. Even criticism and correction can be offered with the attitude of improving the situation.

Having worked directly with young people for a number of years I can tell you that many of them long to hear positive words from a parent. Let's look at the same scenario but with two different approaches.

Approach #1. Your teenager has set a goal of making the basketball team. You go to a practice and see your teen make a couple of bad passes. Afterward your response is something akin to, "Gee, you made of couple of bad passes. You'll need to improve in those areas if you're going to make the team."

Approach #2. Same scenario but your response is, "Gee, you're making some great progress there. What do you feel you're doing well? Where would you like to improve?"

The first response is, of course, true, but not motivating. It will probably close the spirit of your teenager, who already knows about the bad passes and feels the pressure of making the team. All you did was reinforce the pressure.

The second response does two things. First, it's an invitation for you to listen, not give advice. Second, your approach opens their spirit by not condemning but encouraging. They will feel your praise, and you've invited them to discover the truth for themselves.

Your words have power to your teen, and there is often no neutral ground. What you say and the way you say it either feels supportive or demotivating. A life coach that comes alongside is always thinking about the way they're communicating. They focus on praise rather than pessimism.

COACHING EXERCISE
Give your teenager permission to tell you how your words affect them. Tell them you want to be encouraging and ask them to tell you when you're not. Ask them how best you can encourage them even when you have to talk to them about some hard stuff. Remind them that the overall goal is to help them thrive.

COMING ALONGSIDE MEANS TIME

You've heard it said, "It's not the amount of time but the quality." May I respectfully say—*baloney*.

How you spend your time tells you and your teenager what is important in your life. Take a look at your daily planner or PDA. For the most part that will tell you what you value. If your teenager were to look at your schedule, would they see their name there?

Young people who are trying to accomplish something in school, wanting to thrive, need life coaches who will give them their most valuable asset—their time. You don't even have to say anything. Just show up! Be at their games. Their concerts. Their plays. Their practices. Make

> **Time is not only about having your teenager in your schedule, but it's also about being available for them.**

those activities a priority in your schedule. I realize that there will be priorities in your life that sometimes must be done, but generally you can get to a large percentage of your teenager's activities if you just plan accordingly. Believe me, they will notice one way or the other.

I've done a lot of things wrong as a parent. But one thing I did right was to make it a priority to go to my youngest daughter's basketball games. In my job I do a lot of traveling so I had to juggle schedules to make it work. When I walked into the gym my daughter didn't run up to me and scream, "Daddy!" like a six-year-old might have. But I'll guarantee you she knew when I was in the crowd.

Not much was said, but she knew.

Now that I've patted myself on the back, let me tell you something I did wrong. I like to stay busy. Rarely will you find me just sitting down and doing nothing. That sent a wrong signal to my kids. When they wanted to say something to me I would often keep doing what I was doing while trying to listen to them. My distractedness sent the message that what they were saying was not very important. It even happened if they would talk to me on the phone. I simply wasn't giving them my full attention and they noticed. Then they decided, "I'd better not interrupt Dad. He's pretty busy."

The most successful athletic coaches make time for individual players. With the best coaches it is more than just a technique. They genuinely care about the people involved.

It's just another way you communicate, *"I'm about your success."*

COMING ALONGSIDE MEANS OFFERING TANGIBLE SUPPORT

This is a frame of mind that says, *"What can I do to help?"* In some situations you might not be able to do anything. Maybe all you do is listen. But in many cases you can provide something tangible that not only helps your teens but conveys their importance to you and your genuine concern for them.

Let's say one of your daughter's goals is to be in the school play. She specifically wants to be in *West Side Story*, which requires good dancing. But she hasn't done much of that. As her life coach, you've been listening, offering encouragement and going to a

> ***Kids don't care how much you know until they know how much you care.***

rehearsal or two. Now you want to provide something more tangible.

You ask around and find someone who could give your daughter some lessons. You ask your daughter if she'd like to participate. She'll probably need five or six sessions at thirty-five bucks a pop. Maybe you offer to pay the whole deal or say you'll split the cost with her. Even if she doesn't want to take the lessons, your actions have communicated you care. You've spent time trying to find a teacher. You're willing to spend some money. You want to help her succeed.

Tangible support can come in many forms but you've got to be tuned in to even know what might help. They may not acknowledge it, but your teenager will notice that they are higher on your priority list when they see you try-ing to offer support they can see, feel or experience.

COMING ALONGSIDE MEANS TOUCH

The laws of our land now make it very difficult for a caring adult to physically touch a teen. On one hand, that's criti-cally important. On the other hand, it prevents young people from receiving something they crave.

As a parent life coach, however, you don't have to worry about those laws unless, of course, you do something inappropriate. Touching your teen in the right way can convey something that they can't get any other way. There's almost something magical about it.

You have to be wise about when you do it, and it de-pends on the temperament of your child. When your child is angry, it may or may not be the right time for a touch or a hug. For one teenager it may be the perfect thing to help calm him down. For another, it may frustrate her and there-fore make her angrier. You learn this through experience.

But every teenager has a time when a touch will send a message that words can't convey. It can say, "I care." "I un-derstand." "I feel sorry you're facing this." "I believe in you." "I love you." To paraphrase a very old song, "Hug me once, hug me twice and hug me once again."

COACHING QUESTION
When are you comfortable touching your teenager?
When are you uncomfortable?

COMING ALONGSIDE IS ABOUT SERVANTHOOD

The idea of servant leadership is a popular new theme in business circles but an old concept. It was the style of Jesus. Even if you don't share my religious conviction, it's hard to argue with the way Jesus lived. He certainly led, took bold steps and had great dreams, but everything he did was motivated by his desire to serve people. What he did was for them, not for himself.

The job of a servant life coach is to serve your teenager. That doesn't mean you respond to their every wish. It doesn't mean that they're the master and you're the slave. Jesus never modeled it that way. It has a lot more to do with attitude than aptitude.

As a parent life coach you have been given the responsibility of stewardship. You have been given the life of a child. While others will influence, you are the primary caregiver. They will learn most about life from you. Your job is to not only help them thrive in school but to mature into a productive, stable, sufficient adult. It will take your time, your resources, your energy and your heart. But that's what it means to serve.

8

The Universal Law of Little Things

This may be a bit uncomfortable.

Try to imagine your own funeral.

Hymns have been sung. The pastor has given his sermon. Several people have spoken in your honor. They've talked about your accomplishments, your hobbies, your character and perhaps even shared a humorous moment or two. Your children have also asked to speak. They step to the platform.

The crowd feels uneasy. They know this is a difficult and emotional moment for your children. A lump begins to form in many throats.

Through tearful but courageous words, they talk about their dad. How much you loved them. Your good advice. Your fun moments with them. How much they will miss you.

I've been to many funerals and heard those painful and heartfelt expressions of hurt and grief. And I continue to be amazed that when you analyze the comments of those who are closest to the deceased, in many cases the impact the person made on their children did not happen because of some great speech or event. Rather it was the summation of many little things the person did over time. It was the way they laughed or their prayers when they tucked their children in at night. It was the way they looked at their son or daughter when they were proud of them or the kindness they showed toward the elderly woman next door.

The old songwriter was correct. "Little things mean a lot."

I'm about as far away as you can get from being a scientist, but I do understand some of the universal laws of reality. I don't know whether this is in any physics book but I do believe in the law of "little things." Simply stated it means *little actions add up to big impact.*

We not only hear this law in funeral eulogies but we see it in every aspect of life. Computers are made up of hundreds of little parts. So are spaceships, cars, televisions, pianos and your body. Even the chair I am now sitting on as I write is composed of atoms too small for me to see, but they combine with other particles to hold me up.

Having the characteristics of a good life coach is important. Applying principles to help your teenager thrive is also vital. But over time, the little things you do will have the greatest impact.

This concept has a biblical parallel as well. Jesus was quoted in Luke 16:10 as saying, "Whoever can be trusted with very little can also be trusted with much." In this passage he was specifically talking about stewardship, but he demonstrated the connection between small things and big things. He knew that big things, both good and bad, are a result of little actions.

So my last bit of advice for a parent trying to be a good life coach is this: intentionally think about the small things, and then let the big things take care of themselves.

Let me give some examples of little things I think your teenagers will remember.

- Put a note in their books or purse that tells them you're impressed with their goals.

- Phone them when they know you're busy and ask them how they're feeling about a disappointment they just experienced.

- Put your arm around them and whisper in their ear, "I'm glad you're my kid."

- Buy them a small but unexpected gift that you know they would enjoy. It can be as simple as a candy bar you know they like.

- Don't talk down to them when they've done something that disappoints you.

- Ask for their opinion on an issue when you are with your peers.

- Ask for their advice with a problem you are facing.

- Let them drive the car (if they have their license) when they know you'd rather be driving.

Hey, Dads!

Often it's the moms who remember to do these things. That, however, is exactly why they make such a deep impression coming from you.

YOU CAN DO IT

Let's go back to where we started. Life coaching any kid is a tough job. And trying to help them thrive in the school

environment only amplifies the problem. But *you can do it!*
Good coaches, practicing the right principles and under-
standing the law of little things, are being successful every
day. As you look to God for wisdom and regularly pray for
your teenager, you can be successful too.